Blake

&

The Travel Team "Atlanta"

Kahil Cole

Sydnee Newsome-Editor

The Travel Team

Blake is a very curious little girl. She lives with her mom, her dad and her little brother Caleb. She loves science, playing with her friends, but most of all learning about different places around the world. And lucky for her she does all her favorite things all the time. She gets to see her friends almost everyday, her mom is a doctor so she loves science too and her dad travels all over the world for work and shares his fun adventures with Blake.

It's never easy when her dad has to leave for a trip. Blake always gets sad because she knows that she will miss him so much. But she puts on a brave face, because she doesn't want Caleb to be sad too. Blake always gives her dad a big hug right before he leaves. She doesn't want to let go. But he always tells her, "Just like a boomerang, I'm going away from you know, but I'll always come back home."

Even though Blake misses her dad she always loves to hear from him while he's traveling. He always calls or emails Blake and her mom to tell them about the fun things he's doing, and the wonderful places he's seeing while he's away. And for just a little while it feels like they're all experiencing his trip together.

Blake's dad's stories are so fun and exciting that she always shares them with her friends the next day. Anne-Marie, Vaughn and Leah really look forward to Blake filling them in on his travels. They call themselves The Travel Team. One day they want to travel the world together. On his latest trip, Blake's dad is visiting Atlanta, Georgia. Her friends can't wait to hear all about it.

Blake's dad is gone just one day before he calls home. "Hi from the great state of Georgia!" he says when Blake answers the phone. She's so excited to hear from him. He tells her all about what he did that day and Blake can't wait to tell her friends.

"Attention, attention I need The Travel Team over by the tree please." Blake announces. Her friends all come running. "Hi Blake. We can't wait for your first fun story about Atlanta." Leah exclaims. Blake tells her friends all about a very tasty stop that her dad made to the World of Coca Cola. "That's right." says Blake. "An entire building dedicated to soda." She told them about the exhibits highlighting 125 years of Coca Cola history, how you can see the vault that holds the secret soda formula and how her dad took a picture with the Coca Cola Polar Bear. "So cool!" Anne-Marie says.

"Mom, what do you think dad will do today?" Blake asks her mom as they sit down for breakfast. They always try to guess what her dad will do that day before he calls home.

"Maybe he'll go to a Georgia peach farm." Blake's mom says.

"Or maybe he'll visit the University of Georgia and get to see that cute bulldog mascot." Blake says. She can't wait to find out.

14

"Blake, what story do you have for us today?" calls out Vaughn as he, Anne-Marie and Leah are walking into school. Blake starts off by asking her friends if they know what CNN is. "It's the Cable News Network and their main newsroom, and a bunch of their studios, are in Atlanta. My dad got to go on a Behind the Scenes Tour and see how the shows are made and put on TV." Blake explains.

"Sounds fun." says Leah. They're all excited to see what story tomorrow brings.

After her next conversation with her dad Blake can't wait to talk to The Travel Team. They all love animals and will be so excited to hear where he went next. As they walk down the hallway at school the next day, Blake tells them all about her dad's trip to the Georgia Aquarium. "It was amazing!" she says. "They have beluga whales, dolphins, sea lions and the largest fish in the world, the whale shark." Her friends are so impressed and even more so when she tells them that she got to see the whale shark too. "The aquarium has webcams on some of their tanks. My dad was at the aquarium when he called so I jumped on line and we watched the whale shark together." Blake explains. Her friends are so impressed.

18

Blake's dad reminds her when they speak that night that he will be home tomorrow. He is really excited to see Blake, her mom and Caleb. However, he did see one more amazing sight in Atlanta that he is very excited to tell Blake about. The next day Blake meets her friends to play in the park and can't wait to tell them one more story from Atlanta. She starts by telling them that it's about Reverend Martin Luther King Jr. They all learned in school that he was a very important Civil Rights Leader, that he won the Nobel Peace Prize in 1964 and that he was born in Atlanta, Georgia. There is now a bronze statue of him on the grounds of the Georgia Capitol building, honoring him for all the wonderful work he did during his life. "My dad said it was so inspirational and a perfect way to end his trip to Atlanta." Blake says.

Blake tells her friends that she must run because her dad will be home soon. As she walks into her house she calls out for her dad. Her mom lets her know that he isn't home yet, but he should be any time now. Blake waits patiently by the door for what seems like forever when finally, she hears a car outside. She sees the front door start to open and in walks her dad! She is so happy to see him and gives him the biggest hug. He is so happy to be home too.

Blake's dad tucks her into bed that night and gives her a kiss goodnight. She asks him about his next trip coming up. "It won't be until next month sweetie, but I'll be going to Paris, France." he tells her. Blake can't wait to hear all about the amazing things her dad sees next. "And someday," she thinks, as images of Paris run through her head. "Maybe I'll get to join him on one of his trips." She closes her eyes and drifts off to sleep, dreaming of new adventures ahead.

Made in the USA
Columbia, SC
03 March 2021